African Elephants

By Alison Tibbitts and
Alan Roocroft

PUBLISHED BY
Capstone Press
Mankato, Minnesota USA

CIP
LIBRARY OF CONGRESS CATALOGING IN PUBLICATION DATA

Tibbitts, Alison.
    African elephants / by Alison Tibbitts and Alan Roocroft.
        p. cm. -- (Animals, animals, animals)
    Summary: An introduction to the physical characteristics, habits, and
natural environment of the African elephant.

    ISBN 1-56065-100-8
    1. African elephant--Juvenile literature. [1. African elephant.
    2. Elephants.] I. Roocroft, Alan. II. Title. III. Series:
Tibbitts, Alison. Animals, animals, animals.
QL737.P98T53   1992
599.6'1--dc20   92-14795
                                                  CIP
                                                    AC

Consultant:
Alan Roocroft
Manager, Elephant Programs
Zoological Society of San Diego

Photo Credits:
Alison Tibbitts and Alan Roocroft: Cover photo, title page, 3, 5, 7, 9, 10, 17, 18, 21, 22, 25, 27, 28, 32, back cover

Don Kohlbaur: 13, 14

Capstone Press
P.O. Box 669, Mankato, MN, U.S.A. 56002-0669

Sunset casts a soft glow over the **savannah**. A herd of African elephants follows their **matriarch** to open grassland. The enormous ears on the animals look like dark sails drifting in the wind. Babies play near their grazing mothers.

These animals descended from **mammoths** and other **prehistoric** elephants. Their **ancestors** ranged across the Old and New Worlds during the **Ice Age**. Early man was among the first to hunt them fifty thousand years ago. Europe, Asia, and North America contain their **fossil** remains.

Elephants were prized by all the great cultures of the world. They appeared in Egyptian, Greek, and Roman art, books, and decoration. They were given as special gifts to ancient rulers. Their ivory was valued even more than the animals themselves. Their **tusks** were carved into beautiful statues and jewelry.

Ancient armies took elephants into battle. The animals went with Alexander the Great to conquer India and Asia Minor. They climbed over the Alps with Hannibal when he invaded Italy. Crusaders returning from the Middle East told stories about warrior elephants. Ivory was an important part of the slave trade for hundreds of years.

Elephants are highly intelligent. They live in a **complex social structure**. Elephant families have from six to ten mothers, sisters, daughters, and young **calves**. A herd has two or more families. **Bulls** do not live with the herd. They interact with **cows** only for breeding.

The largest and oldest female is the matriarch. She guides and protects her families. She carries in her head the memories needed for the herd's survival. This information has been passed down to her through generations of matriarchs. Experience has taught her where to find food and water. It has shown where dangers wait.

Family life centers around the young. Cows are devoted mothers. The entire herd is aware of the babies. Several come to help if a calf gets into trouble. Each family member has her own scent from birth. Elephants recognize each other by remembering these personal scents.

A single calf is born after nearly two years of development. Twins are rare. The mother chooses a cow without a calf to be with her for the birth. This "auntie" protects mother and calf from **predators** during delivery.

The mother urges her baby to get up and walk within the first hour. Mother, calf and auntie spend a few quiet days before rejoining the family. The others welcome the newcomer by touching and talking to him. The calf lives between his mother's front legs for the first few weeks. Then he comes out to make friends with the others. His mother guides and teaches him.

A female stays with the herd for her lifetime. She begins to breed when she is ten years old. Males are chased from the herd around the age of twelve. The males join a loose-knit bachelor herd or live alone. Later, they compete with older bulls to breed.

The animals take short naps. They lie down to sleep for only a few hours at a time. Looking for food takes eighteen hours a day. They eat grass, bushes, and trees. These grow in forests, woodlands, and open grasslands. Some African elephants have adapted to life in deserts or in dense rainforests.

Elephants balance on their back legs to reach food up high. Leaves and twigs drop to the ground as large branches are broken. Small animals wait for this extra food. Trees will fall over if they are pushed hard enough.

Elephants need lots of water every day. They drink gallons of it. Bath time is a chance to splash and squirt each other as they roll around. They might stay underwater for several minutes. Swimming is natural for elephants. They have been known to go many miles in the open ocean.

These animals are the largest land **mammals**. Males are taller than females. They stand over ten feet tall at the shoulder. Elephants do not see very well. Long, thick lashes protect their eyes from blowing dust. Their flat feet are as wide as basketballs. The tail ends with a bunch of wiry hair. The ears are leather fans which cool the air around them. Blood in the veins behind the ears releases extra body heat.

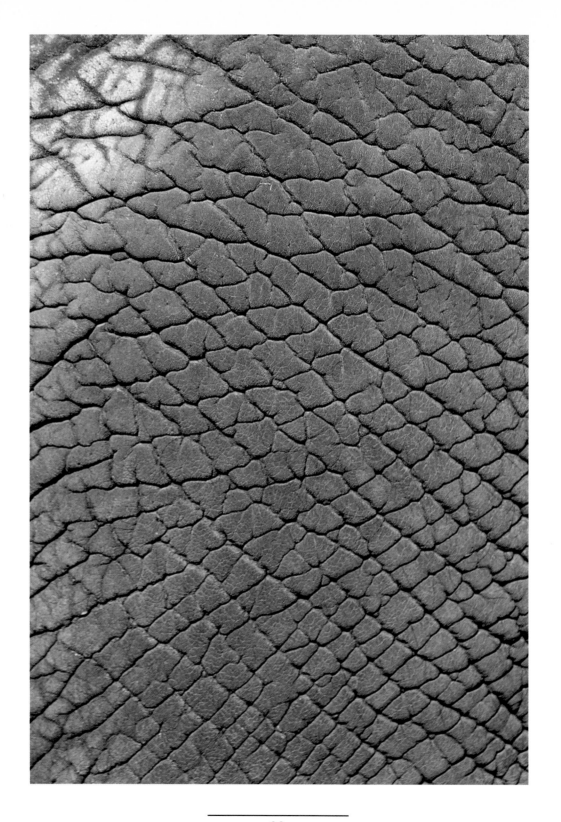

Insects like to hide in elephants' wrinkles. A good dusting protects this sensitive skin from bites and sunburn. The trunk scoops up dirt and blows it over the head and back. Mud is a sunscreen, too.

Tusks are teeth made of a material called ivory. Both male and female African elephants grow these teeth. Tusks do important work. They are used with the trunk to lift or move things. They can be a weapon.

Elephants can find water when there has been no rain. They are able to smell water under the ground. They dig for it with their tusks and feet. This gives water to other animals who cannot dig for themselves.

Trunks are needed for many jobs. They carry things from place to place. They are part of eating, drinking, and scenting. Two sensitive fingers at the end grasp even tiny fruits and nuts. The animals communicate with each other through their trunks.

Affection is important to elephants. They touch, explore, smell, and rub against one another. Their thick skin can feel the lightest touch. They greet each other with loud rumbles, squeaks, trumpets, and bellows.

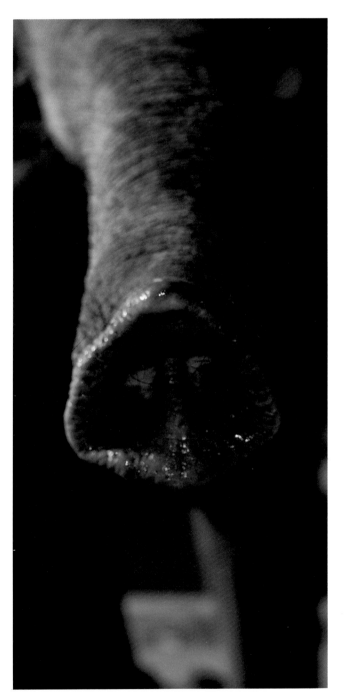

Elephants hear well. They fan their ears straight out to listen. They hold their trunks straight up in the air to sniff when they hear something new. They pick up sounds humans cannot hear. These **infrasounds** travel through the air for miles to tell elephants what is happening. They report about danger, breeding, and what calves are doing.

Today, African elephants live only to the south of the Sahara Desert. Their ivory tusks have become their death warrant in recent years. Poachers have killed half of Africa's elephants and stolen their ivory. In 1989, more than one hundred countries agreed to forbid the sale of ivory. African elephants can survive if people never buy ivory again.

GLOSSARY / INDEX

Ancestors: related animals from whom an animal is descended (page 4)

Bulls: adult males more than ten years old (page 8)

Calves: male and female babies (page 8)

Complex social structure: an organized life in which each member knows his place and role in the family (page 8)

Cows: adult females more than ten years old (page 8)

Fossil: preserved remains, such as bone or tooth, from an animal who lived long ago (page 4)

Ice Age: a period thousands of years ago when sheets of ice covered the Northern Hemisphere (page 4)

Infrasounds: deep sounds too low to be heard by human ear (page 29)

Mammals: animals with a backbone, a four-chambered heart and some hair, who feed their babies milk (page 20)

Mammoths: ancient, hairy elephants who no longer exist (page 4)

Matriarch: female leader of the group (page 3)

Predators: animals who hunt and kill another animal for food (page 15)

Prehistoric: before events were written down as recorded history (page 4)

Savannah: open field with coarse grass and scattered trees (page 3)

Tusks: long, pointed elephant teeth (page 4)